Yorkshire Past

East Riding

Written and compiled by
Stephen Tyndale-Biscoe

First published in 2007 by:
At Heart Ltd, 32 Stamford Street,
Altrincham, Cheshire, WA14 1EY
in conjunction with
Yorkshire Post Newspapers Ltd
PO Box 168, Wellington Street,
Leeds, LS1 1RF

ISBN: 978-1-84547-126-2

Printed and bound by Bell & Bain Ltd, Glasgow

Introduction

The character of East Yorkshire, so different from that of
the other Ridings, is captured on the pages of this book.
Sometimes it seems that the passage of time has hardly
touched the region.

Country towns and villages of great character,
great rivers and the life of agricultural communities
predominate. Then there's Hull, where the mood and
pace of life abruptly alters.

This is a fascinating region, its many aspects explored
over succeeding years by the camera lens as spring,
summer, autumn and winter, ring the seasonal changes.

Written and compiled by Stephen Tyndale-Biscoe, 2007.

Spring

● Telling images that were part of the fabric of life in 1948: a delivery boy with his bicycle and a brewery lorry, laden with barrels of beer. This was the scene in Bridge Street, Tadcaster, on May 12, 1948.

● All was quiet - very quiet indeed - on this bright spring day in Main Street, Ulleskelf, near Tadcaster. The picture was taken on May 20, 1948, and not a soul to be seen.

● Bridge Street, Tadcaster on the March 8, 1948. Before the bypass was built, this street carried all the road traffic between Leeds and York.

● The Falcon Inn on Chapel Street, Tadcaster, May 5, 1948. The truck just beyond it has a single wheel at the front, a not-unusual configuration in the immediate post-war years, and indeed on into the mid-50s.

● The weir and mill at Tadcaster on May 12, 1948.

● Stillingfleet, near Goole in May, 1953, and the only car to be seen appears to be hiding behind a tree on the far side of the bridge, creating a scene that looks almost pre-war. The first mention of a church in Stillingfleet appears in 1244, and in the churchyard is a monument dedicated to 11 members of the church choir who were drowned in 1833, when crossing the River Ouse from Acaster Selby.

● Pleasure rowing boats on the Derwent at Stamford Bridge, early spring, 1958.

● Two boys are mirrored in the water where the river has slowed, one boy fishes while his friend watches, as the Derwent thunders over the weir at Stamford Bridge, in April 1962.

● A pair of heavy horses in train haul timber through
South Dalton, near Beverley, in March 1952.

● The Coastguard Station at Spurn
Point, Humber, May 28, 1980.

● Fishing-cobbles moored at Staithes, March 1990.

● A swirling sea and dramatic coastline
at Staithes on the same day.

● The Humber Tavern in Paull, May 1964.

● Paull Lighthouse on the Humber photographed in May 1964. The lighthouse was built in 1836, but in little more than 50 years a shift in the sandbanks which it was intended to warn against meant it was no longer useful to shipping, and it became a private home. New lights, two at Salt End which fell into disuse, and two more at Thorngumbald Clough, replaced it.

● Although the train tracks are empty the railway crossing in Hull is busy with trucks, cars, bicycles and a scooter. May 1958.

● Anlaby Road Crossing, with St. Matthew's Church
in the background, in Hull, in May 1958.

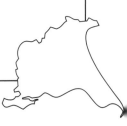

● Queens Gardens, Hull, in 1961
with the Technical College in the
background.

● Hull Docks is a hive of activity, with plenty of trucks being loaded and unloaded, when this picture was taken in 1964.

● George Hales operating a potato planter at
Richard Hile's Low Gardham Farm, East Yorkshire,
covering a 60 acre area. Spring 1972.

● Two sections, which will go towards the creation of the
Humber Bridge, are lowered into place on March 21, 1980.

● Hammonds store in Paragon Square, Hull, after being bombed during the blitz of May 1941. Local historian John Markham published a book tracing the history of the city's famous store.

● The village
pond at Grindale,
Bridlington, being
closely observed by
two companions on
May 25, 1965.

● A general view of Goole, once the only port of the West Riding before the town became part of the East Riding. It was the 10th port of Great Britain and the most inland port of the East Coast of England. This picture was taken on May 26, 1965.

● A close-run thing at Beverley Races in May 1959, but there is little in the way of excited demonstration among the spectators.

● The Bell and Crown pub, in Snaith, advertising local brew Bentley's Yorkshire Bitter. In the background is St. Laurence's church, founded in Saxon times although there is little left of the original building. May 15, 1950.

● The Hull-London train holds up traffic on Boothferry
Road, Goole, on March 24, 1972.

● Goole gets its continental style railway crossing gates. March 2, 1966.

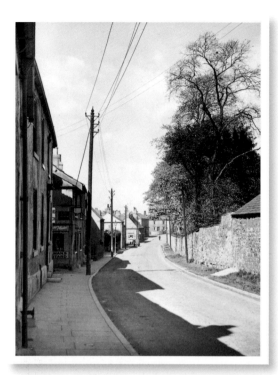

● Main Street, entering the village, Barwick-in-Elmet, from Leeds. April 26, 1949.

● In Barwick-in-Elmet near Leeds an 87ft-tall Maypole is traditionally raised every three years on the Tuesday after the Spring Bank Holiday. It is raised by ladder parties, and when it is up, a volunteer must climb to the top to untie the ropes. This picture of it was taken on April 25, 1949. Lowering the Maypole takes place at Easter.

● A leisurely stroll through Barwick-in-Elmet
on this bright spring day, April 25, 1949.

● Tadcaster, May 12, 1948. Great North Road entering the town from the South. Tadcaster Brewery (John Smiths) on the other side from the road from Sam Smith's Fox and Hounds Inn.

● Chapel Street, Tadcaster, looking west. A Rover has stopped outisde the Falcon Inn on May 13, 1948.

● All Saint's Church and
the Wellington Inn, in Lund,
April 28, 1959.

● Micklefield village, near Selby, May 12, 1975.

● An Earles Cement truck makes its way down Station Road in South Cave, in April 1949.

Summer

● June 29, 1955 and three cyclists make
their way through Airmyn, near Goole,
and are not too concerned about the
traffic. Airmyn, near to where the River
Aire flows into the Ouse, is really too
large to be a proper village, and in the
Middle Ages it was a small port.

● A calm August day in 1964, and only a boat can continue the journey from where the path ends at the water's edge at Airmyn.

There was a time when those who died in Airmyn were taken by boat to be buried in Snaith, the journey by boat being quicker than by horse and cart.

● The Ouse near Airmyn on the same August day, and poplars line the bank as still as sentries.

● "The Old Ark", the oldest house in Tadcaster, as it looked on August 10, 1942. The house dates from the late 15th Century, and has been enlarged and altered numerous times over the succeeding centuries, and is reputedly where the Pilgrim Fathers met when planning their voyage to America.

In 1959 it was in danger of demolition when Mr W H D Riley-Smith decided that the town's oldest house should be preserved for the public, and a major restoration programme was begun. The building seen in this photograph is barely recognisable today.

● Listed buildings in Mytongate, Hull, and in a very sorry state.

● This photo was taken from the balcony of the tower at Spurn Point in the summer of 1951. In the foreground, enclosed by a high wall to keep out drifting sand and bad weather, are the houses of the 'Keepers.

● The year is 1971 and Hammond's of Hull - "more than a shop, it is an institution" - celebrated its 150th anniversary. Despite the elaborate celebrations, which included a visit from Princess Margaret, the origins of the business are somewhat veiled. A directory of 1831, however, records the existence of H W Hammond's first shop in North Bridge.

● Houses being demolished on Marmaduke
Street, near Hessle Road, Hull.

● The statue of Queen Victoria in City Square, Hull, in 1957, and the
overhead trolley bus powerlines seen here are long since gone.

● Hull Docks in 1972, near the point where
the River Hull meets the Humber.

● Paull Lighthouse was built in 1836, and fell
into disuse by the end of the 19th Century.
This picture was taken on June 12, 1950.

● A picture of seaside bliss. This is the August bank holiday in 1957, and Mr Harold Helliwell of Bradford enjoys an ice cream as he relaxes on the sands at Bridlington.

● The British Cocoa Mills factory
and Wharf on the River Hull, in Hull.

● Selby Shipyards launching of the "*Lady Elizabeth*". The yard built a wide range of vessels including bulk carriers, Rhine Traders with telescopic wheel houses to negotiate low bridges, the Isle of Wight Ferry and large trawlers. William Edgar CBE, in his presidential address to the Institution of Mechanical Engineers, which he delivered in May 2004, recalled his time from 1988 to 1990 as Executive Chairman of Cochrane Ship Builders. By that stage, he said, the Selby business had had a chequered history, but possessed one of the best work forces he had ever had to work with. The quality of the vessels at Cochranes was superb, and launching them was, he said, exciting since it was a sideways launch into the River Ouse, 72 miles from the open sea.

● A weights and measures inspector makes notes
at one of the stalls at the open market at Melbourne
Airfield, Pocklington, June 2, 1973.

● Mr George Morton's 138-acre farm near Holme-on-Spalding-Moor
in the East Riding. The farm was one of the last farms to still be
using shire horses in 1971.

● A reassuring hand for a reluctant swimmer at Flamborough in June 1960.

● A tractor hauls a fishing-cobble across
the sand at Filey, July 1960.

● Members of the sailing club with their dinghies
on the shore at Filey, June 22, 1962.

● The Spread Eagle Inn on Exchange Street, in Driffold, on August 28, 1947.

● A Coronation Day parade outside Bridlington Spa.

● A lone cyclist makes his way down Hengate, Beverley, on August 29, 1947.

● The tower of St. Mary's Church, in Beverley, said to be one of the most beautiful churches in England, collapsed in 1520 and fell on the nave killing several people. This is St. Mary's as it looked on August 9, 1946.

● Beverley Minster, August 28,1953.

● Racehorses training on Beverley Westwood, Beverley, August 1960.

● Lotherton Hall Chapel, Aberford, 1938. The little chapel at Lotherton dates from the late 12th Century and served as a Chapel-of-Ease to Sherburn-in-Elmet. The simple oblong nave and lower chancel are built of coursed rubble and the chapel's setting, in front of a group of trees close to the hall, enhances its visual appeal.

• Spurn Point, as pictured here, is on the north bank of the entrance to the River Humber estuary.

● An almost deserted street outside the White Swan
in Sherburn in Elmet, July 1953.

Autumn

● A giant turnip wins a delighted smile from a turnip puller on a farm at Sherburn-in-Elmet in October 1950.

● Turnip pullers bend to their task, attended by a child too
young to be left at home, and too young for school.

● Delivery DUKWs, Army amphibious vehicles, were used to ferry supplies around Selby in 1947.

● Paull, November 1957. Paull lighthouse on the Humber.

● Unchanged since the early years of the century, Sunnybank in Micklefield near Selby, photographed on September 27, 1979.

● A new perspective of the Guildhall, Hull, was provided by the demolition of Queen's Hall in 1965.

● Hull prison on October 27, 1958. "The senior inmates" it was reported "are allowed periods of moving about the Borstal without strict supervision. Here one is mowing the lawn."

● Goole's clock tower in the town centre, photographed on September 4, 1958. It was erected in 1927 as part of the celebrations marking 100 years since the opening of the docks. The clock tower replaced a large gas lamp that had been there previously.

● October 28, 1946, and smoke drifts from the stacks of the coal barge *Doreen* which has just made a delivery to Ferrybridge Power Station.

● Scarborough's Grand Hotel looms large behind a crowded beach, on a warm late October day, 1960.

● Ferrybridge Power Station, October 29, 1946.

● Boothferry Road, town centre, in Goole on
September 5, 1958.

● The pleasure boat *Primrose* leaves the sanctury of Bridlington harbour with high-spirited passengers on board in September 1958.

● A street scene in Driffield, captured by the camera on September 2, 1950.

● A description of All Saint's, in Driffield, published in 1892 states that it is "a stately and well-proportioned edifice, of which its tower is its glory. It is all that a tower should be - simple and massive in its early stages, and then leading the eye up to dignified enrichment, which fitly crowns it and breaks the sky-line." This picture of the Parish Church was taken on a bright November day in 1947.

● St. Helen's Church, in Stillingfleet, was constructed in Norman times (c.1150-1160) by Robert de Stutville. November 14, 1945.

● Fallen leaves - the perennial price for autumn's gorgeous colours. Here, in October 1954, they are being swept up in Beverley.

● Pocklington, the level crossing and beyond it the Parish Church of All Saints, September 21, 1958.

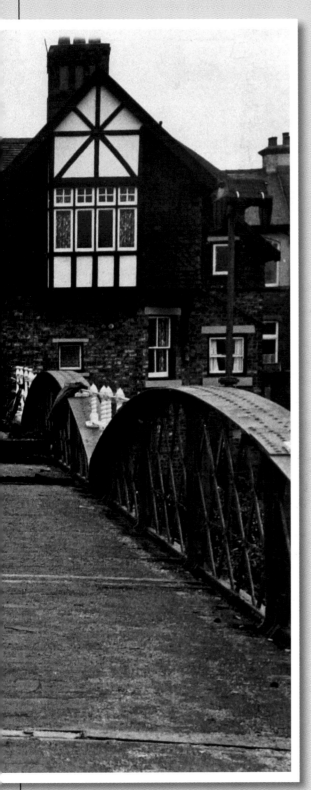

● Work in progress on the bridge at Cawood, September 20, 1973.

Winter

● The snow which had fallen not long before is melting, as a horse which has no need of guidance pulls a cart and its two passengers through Saxton, near Tadcaster, on January 16, 1952.

● Spurn Point, February 7, 1977. Since 1960 it has been owned by the Yorkshire Wildlife Trust and is a designated National Nature Reserve, Heritage Coast and is part of the Humber Flats, Marshes and Coast Special Protection Area.

● Another view of Spurn Point, taken on February 7, 1977.

● A familiar enough sight on the Holderness coast,
here the wave damage is at Spurn, in February 1953.

● On January
10, 1982, an
extraordinary scene
as packed ice
surrounds a frozen
car in Bondgate,
Selby.

● Hull City Hall, December 1952.

● A night scene in December,
1963, looking across the
Queen's Gardens, Hull, towards
the Technical College.

● High and dry - repairs to the Banquo deep-sea trawler in a Hull dock, November 1961. She was eventually scrapped in Ghent.

● The visit of *HMS Wakefield* to Hull in November 1964.

● After a heavy snow fall in the winter of 1960, an RAF helicopter
hovers over drivers struggling to free some of the trapped cars
and buses, which had been abandoned near Grindale a few miles
north of Bridlington, the previous night.

● October 31, 1965, and the remains of two cooling towers at Ferrybridge Power Station which had been demolished by gale-force winds.

● Barges bring coal to the power station on a cold February day in 1954.

● Mr. Tom Hunt uses a boat to ferry people across High Street in the floods at Cawood, near Selby, on January 6, 1982.

● Mr. Alfred Teal at work in the Old Red Brick Smithy,
Lund, East Yorkshire, on January 24, 1973.

● A trainer treats one of his charges to a bottle of Guinness.

● A race horse is shod at the King's Arms Stables, Beverley, in January 1965.

● Crossing North Bar Within, race horses from the stables are taken out to be exercised.

● Grade II listed St.
David's Church in Airmyn,
near Goole, December
1953.

● Skidby Mill, between Hull and Beverley, is Yorkshire's last working windmill. It dates from 1821 when it was built for a Mr Watson. In 1966 it was sold to the Beverley Borough Council for a nominal charge of £1. This photo of the mill was taken on December 8, 1973.